Anger Management

How to Tame Your Angry Mood, Take Charge of Your Emotions, and Get Rid of Stress and Anxiety Complete with Helpful Advice on Improving Your Self-Control

Johann Renner

TABLE OF CONTENT

The Harmful Consequences Of Ongoing Angry Behavior 1

The Emotion That Is Often Misunderstood 10

Reorganization Based On Sound Logic 25

Definitions And Categories Of Angry Feelings 30

What Exactly Is The Meaning Of The Term "Anger Management"? 50

Managing Anger In The Presence Of Complete Strangers 68

You May Trace Each Of These Things Back To The Origin Of Your Anger... Take Good Care Of Them To Prevent Them From Throwing It Away. 72

Sign Up For A Class On Managing Your Angry Moods. 81

What Kind Of Experience Should You Have When Visiting A Professional Counselor Or Medical Doctor? 87

What Exactly Is The Concept Of Parenting Triggers? 98

What Exactly Are The Issues With Controlling One's Anger? 105

How To Stay Away From Tantrums 114

When Should You Start To Be Worried? 118

The Most Pervasive Misconceptions Regarding Angry Behavior.. 145

The Influence Of Having Compassion For Oneself.. 160

The Harmful Consequences Of Ongoing Angry Behavior

The Buddha is considered to be one of the brightest persons to have ever lived; the vast majority of the advice that he provided is undeniably accurate. You may want to use your anger to damage someone who has caused you grief, but the longer you hold onto that anger, the more it burns you. The Buddha is correct when he says that anger burns you the most before it burns the person you are furious at. In the quotation above, the Buddha says that anger burns you the most before it burns the person you are upset at. Your mind, body, and life are all in for a world of hurt if you let your anger fester for extended periods of time, particularly if you internalise it and turn it against yourself.

Before we go into the specifics of the numerous tactics that are shown to be beneficial for anger management, let's first go over all of the reasons why you should make it a priority to improve your ability to regulate your emotions, with a particular focus on your ability to control your anger.

Fury makes your heart less strong.

rage that is occasional and warranted is reasonable, and such episodes of rage do not negatively impact a person's body or health. On the other hand, your outbursts of anger are only doing harm to your heart if they are frequent and powerful. According to Chris Aiken, MD, a clinical psychiatry teacher at the Wake Forest University School of Medicine, your risk of experiencing a cardiac arrest increases by a factor of two in the two hours after an outburst of rage.

He also discusses how repressed anger, which is when you attempt to control your anger, bottle it up, and express it indirectly, increases your chance of suffering from heart disease. He defines repressed anger as "when you try to control your anger, bottle it up, and express it indirectly." According to the findings of a recent research, people who have anger as a character feature are at a greater risk of developing cardiovascular disease than their contemporaries who have a temperament that is less fiery.

It raises the likelihood of you having a stroke.

According to the findings of a research, those who are prone to lashing out have a three times increased chance of having a stroke two hours following an incident of rage. This increased risk may be due to bleeding inside the brain or due to a blood clot in the brain. If a person has an aneurysm in their brain, the probability of it rupturing rises by a factor of six following an outburst of anger.

It has a detrimental effect on your immune system.

According to the findings of a study that was carried out by experts from Harvard, if a healthy individual remembers earlier experiences of anger, he or she suffers a 6-hour decrease in the levels of the antibody immunoglobulin A. This is because immunoglobulin A is the first line of defence that our cells have against any illness. This indicates that even thinking about a period when you were furious is enough to impair your immune system, and if you are someone who easily loses their temper, it is probable that your rage outbursts will cause damage to your immune system that will worsen over time.

exacerbates feelings of worry and stress

Your levels of worry and tension will escalate with each outburst of fury you have if you are someone who is always worried about things. One's symptoms of generalised anxiety disorder (GAD), a disease in which one worries excessively and uncontrolled, might be made worse by anger, according to the findings of a research that was published in 2012. Because anger causes cortisol levels to surge, those who are prone to anxiety and chronic stress may experience a worsening of their symptoms both during and after encounters with fury. The production of cortisol is the hormone that is most closely linked to the regulation of stress levels inside the body.

Contributes to the onset and severity of depression

The link between sadness and rage, especially in males, has been shown by a number of research conducted over the course of time. Depression is a common side effect of a kind of rage known as passive anger, in which the person keeps ruminating about the source of their anger but never really acts on it and keeps it bottled up for a lengthy period of time. Because you keep worrying about all of the things that disturb you, which may stir up irritation and rage, depression can also lead to passive anger. This happens when you keep thinking about all of the things that annoy you. Whether sadness causes anger or vice versa, the two have a negative impact on a person's health, well-being, and capacity to live a happy life.

It is harmful to your lungs.

Anger is a negative habit that, like smoking, is harmful to your lungs. However, anger is more detrimental to your lungs than smoking is. Over the course of eight years, researchers from Harvard University evaluated 670 adult males and assessed the amount of animosity in each participant using a hostility scale. The findings demonstrated that the males who were rated as having the greatest levels of hostility also had a reduced lung capacity and were more likely to have respiratory issues. The researchers also hypothesised that anger was induced by a surge in stress hormones such as cortisol, which in turn contributed to inflammation in the lungs' airways. This theory was supported by the findings.

Reduces the length of your life span.

A life marred by persistent stress is an unhealthy existence. According to the findings of a research that was carried out by the University of Michigan, married couples who have a pattern of repressing their anger have a tendency to have a lower life duration in comparison to those who do not repress their anger. Passive anger and other forms of rage, when harboured for an excessive amount of time, may lead to depression, other mental problems, and physical health concerns that harm your health and shorten your lifetime. Passive anger is anger that is not directly directed at another person.

Problems for relationships are caused by this.

Chronic anger, in addition to causing negative effects on one's health, may also set the stage for strained interpersonal interactions. It is only going to hurt and destroy your relationships if the people who are important to you regard you as someone who is "a constant time bomb," someone who is inclined to anger easily, often, and to act out their anger in explosive ways. As long as you keep "exploding" at other people, nobody will want to be near you. This will have a negative impact on your romantic life as well as your other relationships, leaving you feeling depressed and lonely.

The Emotion That Is Often Misunderstood

Anger, out of all the other feelings that a person is capable of having, is the one that might be the most difficult to pinpoint in the present moment. When you're in an upset mood, you could have the impression that you've never before had such a clear picture of the world around you. But you do have control over how you react to it, a power that many people give up as an excuse to do something violent or harmful and then not accept responsibility for their actions after the fact. Anger is an emotion, and as such, you have no actual control over when you experience it. However, you do have control over how you respond to it.

individuals who struggle with anger difficulties often make the mistake of writing it off without thinking about the numerous ways in which anger can also be a good energy. Unfortunately, anger is sometimes grouped in with violence and aggressiveness, and individuals who struggle with anger frequently make this mistake. As a result, the purpose of this chapter is to educate you on the feeling that is the most misunderstood in order to get you started on the path to improving your relationship with that feeling once and for all.

Discontent is multifaceted.

To a large number of people, anger and aggressive behaviour are synonymous terms. However, this is more of a reflection on the individuals who hold these beliefs than it is on the emotion itself. The majority of people grossly underestimate the complexity and range of expressions that anger may take. In point of fact, anger spans a wide range of emotions, from the moderate aggravation that a person may experience when they stub their toe to the all-consuming wrath that a person can feel when their pet is run over by a person who is on their smartphone. Anger can range from mild frustration to intense rage.

aggressiveness is its own independent behaviour that contains a very clear desire to do physical or verbal damage to a person or object. While anger and aggressiveness often go hand in hand, it is important to note that aggression is a separate and different behaviour from anger. It is vital to grasp the difference if you are now dealing with anger difficulties of any kind or another because doing so is the first step towards taking back some of the power that you have no doubt given this feeling. If you are currently dealing with anger issues, it is important to understand the distinction because doing so is the first step towards taking back some of the power. It's possible that right now you have the impression that when you become furious, the anger takes control, making you a reluctant participant in whatever happens after that. This could not be farther from the truth, however, and the remainder of this book will teach you how you may find how to control the result of your actions or inactions and how you can do so by discovering how to control the outcome of your actions or inactions.

It is easy to anticipate anger.

When a person is confronted with a circumstance that they perceive to be either unjust or unpleasant, it is reasonable to assume that they will experience feelings of anger. After that, you can depend on them to get more angry if there is someone around whom they can blame for their dilemma, or if it is obvious that the problem could have been avoided in the first place. Both of these things are certain ways to make them even more irate. If it is reasonable to assume that the majority of individuals would respond in the same manner when shown the same set of criteria, then the issue that arises is why certain people become so much angrier so much more often than others.

The answer to this question is that everyone has a distinct cutoff point that they use to determine whether or not these requirements have been reached. Those who struggle to control their anger have, for one reason or another, acquired the habit of going to extremes nearly as soon as the opportunity arises. This is because they have learned that this is the only way to get what they want. For instance, if someone cuts in front of you in queue at the grocery store, you have the option of assuming that they did it on purpose, which is guaranteed to provoke anger, or you may think that they didn't notice you, which opens the scenario up to a variety of alternative possibilities. Either way, your reaction is certain to be negative.

Those who prefer to believe the first assumption rather than the second may not even be aware that there is a choice in the issue. This is one of the reasons why it may be so challenging for a lot of people to accept the fact that they have an anger problem in the first place. However, if they realise that not everyone feels anger in the same way that they do, then it will be possible to make greater progress; however, this will only be the case if they are prepared to work towards achieving this goal. This type of thing can only come about with a lot of hard effort and devotion to succeeding in the long-term, so it is vital to keep in mind that this kind of change cannot be done overnight. It is crucial to keep in mind that no change to something as big as the way rage is experienced can be achieved overnight.

Manifestations of wrath on the body

Anyone who has ever experienced extreme rage is aware that it is possible for very genuine bodily symptoms to emerge as a consequence of the experience. When you're angry, your feelings go into overdrive, and as a result, your whole body starts to experience the effects of that, as well as exhibit them. It's not only in your thoughts; anger may manifest itself in very physical ways, both on the inside and the exterior of your body. Take a look at some of the bodily manifestations that are linked to rage, including the following:

Pain in the head

Uneasy and rapid heartbeats

a state of exhaustion

Tingling sensations

The pressure that was exerted on the sinus cavities

Unhealthy levels of blood pressure

Are any of these symptoms anything you're acquainted with? When you become furious, do you find that you are able to recall experiencing any of those emotions? Do you believe it's natural for you to experience your anger not only emotionally, but also physically? What does this imply about the emotion of anger? First and foremost, it demonstrates how formidable rage can be. It is an all-consuming sensation that has the potential to quickly take control of you if you let it. In addition to the fact that it does not depend on logic, it also forces you to behave in a way that you would not ordinarily act.

Manifestations of fury on an emotional level

The common misconception is that the emotional symptoms of anger are really greater anger. This is not the case. In point of fact, they may include a wide variety of symptoms, ranging from irritation and anxiety to sadness. If you bottle up your anger and don't find another way to release it, it may grow into a much more significant emotional problem that has long-lasting impacts on your psychology and mental health. Your frustration may have been sparked by a genuine issue that has persisted for a long time and that you have not addressed and are unable to fix. This feeds anxiety and generalised anger, both of which may lead to self-inflicted injury.

Repercussions of being angry

The negative consequences of rage may sometimes be much more harmful than the emotion itself. The incorrect display of rage may have repercussions not only on a person's mental but also on their physical health. When I was having trouble dealing with my anger, for instance, the only thing that seemed to help was to try to stifle it as much as possible. I had no idea that I was just going to end up causing additional difficulties for myself by doing that. You are under the impression that showing your anger is wrong, but were you aware that keeping it bottled up is an even worse problem?

It's accurate to say that anger is a normal human emotion, and it's important to find appropriate ways to express it. If you don't confront it, the underlying source of that fury will continue to eat away at you, sometimes literally. If you don't address it, it will continue to rot away at you. Because of my anxiousness, I ended up having troubles that were connected to my stomach. I was unknowingly contributing to my own illness by choosing to repress my anger rather than letting it out. Where do you believe the expression "worried sick" originated?

And that's just the list of the physical side effects, which I, along with so many other people, was forced to endure. However, you should be aware that there are also actual impacts on your mental health that might arise as a result of this. Mental health issues like anxiety and depression may manifest themselves or get worse if you don't get help. In turn, this may lead to concerns such as drug misuse, heart disease, digestive troubles, high blood pressure, sleeping problems, the flu, heart attacks, and even cancer.

The significance of seeking assistance when needed

As you can see, rage is nothing to make light of, and it is capable of causing some very significant difficulties. No matter how you express it—by lashing out or by bottling it up—anger can and will do damage on both the inside and the outside of a person. To put this into perspective, this is precisely why you should address any problems linked to anger that you may have before it is too late and they have already managed to damage your health.

Learning how to communicate your frustration in an appropriate manner is of equal importance. Keeping everything to oneself may seem to be the best course of action, particularly when one is in public. Nobody wants to be the one to start a scene or make other people feel awkward or uncomfortable in a social setting. But denying your anger and keeping your bad feelings bottled up within can do nothing but hurt you in the long term, even if you aren't aware of this fact just yet. You can't let go of the past and pretend it never happened. Believe me when I say that suppressing your feelings and keeping them bottled up within is not going to serve you well in any way, shape, or form.

In addition, despite the fact that rage is often illogical, this does not imply that it is never warranted. I am aware that it does not make any sense, but please give me a moment of your time to explain. I believe that there are certain circumstances that need an extreme response, and we can all agree on that. Consider the possibility that a close friend may betray you by exposing in public a personal confidence that you have shared with them. You have every right to be upset with them since they have mistreated you and their behaviour has been appalling. Everyone in this world would agree with you that you have every right to be furious with them.

Not shouting at someone may be the courteous thing to do, but it is not the healthy thing to do. Showing restraint by not yelling at them is not the healthy thing to do. If you don't let out your anger, it won't go away; instead, it will fester deep inside you, eating away at your physical and mental well-being until it finally explodes. If you don't express your anger, it won't go away. You will continue to feel angry, but instead of lashing out in a fit of rage and having the issue resolved once and for all, you will bear your anger in silence and may even come to despise your buddy. Keeping your anger bottled up may have negative effects on your a) physical health, b) mental health, and c) connection with the person you are feeling furious against.

Reorganization Based On Sound Logic

Altering the manner in which you think is another effective method that may be used to help you get control of your emotions and prevent you from engaging in violent behaviours. The person has to acquire the following knowledge in order to have any chance of being successful while applying such a method:

Figure out how to change their negative "inner dialogues" into a more upbeat and optimistic one. When a person is furious, their ideas have a greater propensity to become exaggerated to an unreasonable degree. You may adjust your ideas to be more encouraging such as saying to yourself, "Yes, it is a frustrating situation. You are not skilled enough to make it happen the way you want it to," instead of believing that "Everything isn't just happening the way you want it because you are not skilled enough to make it happen." Nevertheless, the fact that you are aware of your shortcomings is a fantastic beginning point, and you will know what aspects of yourself need to be improved in order to achieve your goals.

Reminding yourself on a consistent basis that being upset will not assist you in overcoming the issue, and that it may potentially make things worse, is an important step to take. This will train your thoughts to always look for answers rather than making excuses or complaining about the situation.

When you're in an upset mood, try to restrain yourself from using words like "always" and "never," as in "You're always late in submitting your work."

Because of this, the other person is less likely to want to collaborate with you and think of a solution.

Always allow reason to triumph over your reasoning. People have a propensity to behave irrationally, particularly when the intensity of their emotions is high. You will be able to take a more objective look at the circumstance if you focus on "thinking" rather than "feeling" about it. If you just follow what your feelings tell you to do, this information may help you make decisions that are more acceptable. In this way, you will never lose control of the situation since you will consciously be in charge of it rather than the other way around.

Develop your ability to communicate more effectively.

People will always need to directly confront the source of the issue if they want it to be remedied in any manner, and there is no way around this need. And when someone is really upset, they have a tendency to make hasty judgements. Nevertheless, being in this position not only fixes the existing issue, but it also has the potential to generate a new problem, one that may even have a personal basis. As a result, it is essential to be aware of the appropriate ways to communicate rage. You may improve this ability by paying attention to the following points:

Learn how to slow down because, given that anger often leads to violence, it is likely that they will send the message that they are aggressive if they let their emotion to take control of them.

Therefore, it is recommended that the individual learn how to "think twice" so that they will not say the first thing that comes to their mind, which is likely to be offensive. This will prevent them from making a statement that they will later regret. Try to keep in mind that the confrontation is about more than just you.

In a same vein, educate yourself on how to listen carefully. If you retain an open mind, you will reduce the likelihood that you may hear things in a selective manner. You will be better able to comprehend their position as a result, and you will be in a position to respond appropriately.

Figure out how to communicate without resorting to fighting back. Even if it may take some time before you convey your point (or understand the other person's perspective), doing so is still preferable than allowing the conversation to spiral out of control as a result of being too defensive.

Definitions And Categories Of Angry Feelings

Anger is an emotion that is connected to an individual's internal perception of having been insulted, mistreated, or rejected, as well as a predisposition to respond by engaging in retribution. Anger is an emotion that consists of a powerful and unpleasant emotional reaction to anything that is thought to have provoked it.

Anger is the desire to vocalise one's discontent with anything that has been spoken about them or that has been done to them. A strong sense of discontent, anger, or hate towards someone or something, often paired with a need for revenge. It is an emotional expression of dissatisfaction; a strong feeling of displeasure, hostility, or hatred against someone or something.

There are two distinct manifestations of rage. Both "holy" and "unholy" fury are terms that I like to use to describe them. Anger, both positive and negative. Yes. Not all instances of wrath are bad or wicked. Joyce Meyer once asked, "Is it wrong to be angry sometimes? No, although a portion of it is true. Even God feels justifiable rage when it comes to things like immorality, injustice, disobedience, and pettiness. Since one might find a positive use for anger on sometimes, one cannot always consider it to be a vice.

Righteous indignation is a term used to describe an appropriate kind of wrath. It is "typically a reactive emotion of anger over mistreatment, insult, or malice," and it may be caused by any of those three things. It is comparable to something that is referred to as "the sense of injustice." (Source: Wikipedia)

"God is a judge who is completely fair, and he is furious with the wicked on a daily basis," says the Bible. Psalm 7:11 (The Message)

The wrath of God is not directed at individual people; if it were, all of humanity would have perished long ago. His rage is directed against the evil deeds that people do against one another on a regular basis.

There were a few occasions when Jesus displayed his wrath. But the injustice that He saw in the world and the callousness of the people made Him very angry. And he [Jesus] replied to them, "Is it lawful on the Sabbath to do good or to do harm, to save life or to kill?" The question comes from a passage in the Bible. However, they did not speak up. And with rage in his eyes, he glanced about at them, grieving over the callousness of their hearts, and then he said to the man, "Stretch out your hand." He then extended it, and the use of his hand was returned to him. - Mark 3:4-5

Jesus travelled up to Jerusalem because the Jewish festival of Passover was getting close to starting. Inside the temple, he discovered people who were trading oxen, lambs, and pigeons for money, as well as other people who were selling other animals.

He then fashioned a whip out of cords and used it to drive everyone, including the sheep and oxen, out of the sanctuary. In addition to this, he tipped over the tables where the money was being exchanged and spilled out the coins.

And he said to the people who were selling the pigeons, "Take these things away; do not make my Father's house a house of trade."

On day 11, you should make it a point to avoid confrontations.

When you say you want to avoid fights, this does not only imply getting yourself out of conflicts; it also involves avoiding allowing yourself to watch fights, whether they are shown on screen, played out in sports, or sung about in music with angry or defiant lyrics. If you can help it, stay away from violent films and music since they will only encourage your inclination to overreact even to relatively little annoyances. According to a number of studies, exposure to violent content in the media might make people more belligerent and insensitive. You won't be able to better control your anger as a result of this consequence in any manner.

If you take the time to educate yourself on the indicators that a confrontation is about to occur, you will be able to take measures to mitigate the negative consequences that will inevitably follow. Putting one's hands on one's hips, squaring one's feet as if they are ready to get into a fight, or jutting out one's chin in a defiant manner are all likely signals that another party is about to transition from being uneasy to outright furious.

If any of these nonverbal indicators are present, it is imperative that you do all in your power to de-escalate the situation.

In this scenario, the most effective method to get things started is for you to make use of a lot of open and submissive nonverbal indicators of your own in addition to a calm voice to signal that you are open to coming to an agreement that is good to both parties.

The easiest method to find out whether the other party is presently at ease is to give them the opportunity to gauge how much space there is between the two of you for the purpose of the interaction that is now taking place. You will be able to get a better sense of how the engagement as a whole is going by observing the amount of physical space that is maintained between you and the other person, particularly if you let them to choose the distance at the beginning of the discussion. The same thing may be stated if they begin the discussion by holding something or otherwise establishing a physical barrier between you: the more successfully the engagement is continuing, the less obstacles there should be.

It is vital to have a concept of all the possible red signals for discomfort so that when you meet one, you can guide the contact back towards more comfortable seas. While everyone reacts to discomfort differently, it is necessary to have an understanding of what all the potential red flags for discomfort are. Along with the indicators of discomfort itself, it is vital to have a clear sense of how serious the nonverbal signal is as well. This is because knowing how severe the nonverbal signal is may be the difference between changing one's course of action and saving one's face and fleeing the area and praying for the best.

Rubbing or caressing the back of the neck repeatedly is one of the most obvious subconscious signals of pain, and the more often someone does this, the more uncomfortable they are. Touching this area, which has a high concentration of nerve endings, may actually slow down your pulse rate, making it look as if you are doing an activity that is more subconscious than it really is. If the other person is wearing anything around their neck, fidgeting with that item is another indication that they are feeling uneasy. The act of crossing one's arms or turning one's body in such a manner as to seem more off from you is a less significant indicator. An increase in frowning or a wrinkled brow are two of the most subtle signals that a person is growing uncomfortable; thus, you should check for these facial expressions. If any of these warning signals appear, you should end the discussion you're having or create an excuse to leave the room.

The Meaning of the Word "Anger"

It is quite difficult to put one's finger on exactly what fury is. People have a tendency to answer the question "what is anger?" by describing the circumstances or triggers that cause them to become furious, or by describing how they feel when they are angry. This demonstrates that rage is an entirely internal and subjective experience. Something that sets another person on fire with wrath could not make any sense to them at all.

Consequently, if you come across a person who is acting irrationally because they failed to purchase smokes before going out for the evening and all of the stores were already closed, you may not understand what's going on. Again, if you are becoming irritated because the family living next door to you is playing music at a loud volume, it is possible that they do not understand why you are unable to take pleasure in listening to high-quality music while they are able to do so.

One definition of rage is that it is "a strong feeling of displeasure and belligerence aroused by a wrong; wrath; ire."

(available on Dictionary.com)

Causes for Being Angry

Since it is difficult to really describe anger, let's take this opportunity to investigate the factors that contribute to it, also known as the causes of anger or the reasons we get angry in the first place.

It's possible that you're irritated when:

You are harmed and are experiencing bodily discomfort right now.

You are starving, but you do not have any food readily available or at your chosen location.

You discover that you have been the target of a criminal act, such as stealing, robbery, abuse, rape, etc.

You are experiencing anxiety because you are stalled in traffic or in a very lengthy line.

You are going through a very difficult time of loss, such as the loss of a loved one.

You are experiencing sexual dissatisfaction.

You are going through the process of detoxing from an addiction, such as drugs, alcohol, or sexual activity.

You have been lied to or cheated on, and you are experiencing difficulties in your romantic relationships as a result.

You are completely spent or worn out You have recently been subjected to impolite or unsavoury conduct

You are frustrated and have no control over the situation.

You get the impression that someone else is exercising authority over you.

You are feeling the heat at work, whether it be from a demanding supervisor or an impending deadline.

You are currently dealing with a financial emergency or debt.

You are experiencing feelings of disappointment in both yourself and other people.

As I said earlier, life will offer you plenty of reasons to be angry, but are you aware of the damage that holding onto anger for too long may do to your life?

Keep an eye on how you carry yourself. It is just as crucial to keep an eye on what your hands and body are doing as it is to monitor what you say. Body language may sometimes be what differentiates someone who is exerting themselves (with a loud and harsh voice) from someone who is just angry. It's possible that when you're talking to someone, you're performing any one of the following things without even realising it:

A really impolite gesture that involves pointing towards the other person.

clenching your teeth nervously between each syllable

Throwing your hand or anything else violently against the table or another surface.

Making a fist with your hand

Other people will see these and other "angry habits" as warning signs that you've lost control of your anger. Maintaining your composure will give you a higher chance of being able to regulate how you respond to different situations. When you're feeling furious, it's crucial to keep an eye on a few specific areas of your body, including the following:

Facial expression is incredibly expressive, yet it may be managed so that other people do not believe you have lost your anger.

When individuals converse, their hands are often moving around quite a bit.When the individual is furious, they have a greater tendency to move about.

Even if it's not technically a part of your body, physical space is nonetheless an essential component of the language that's used. When you chat to someone, projecting an aggressive demeanour is helped along by standing too near to them. Make an effort not to be in the other person's face too much.

The tenor of one's voice is something that needs no explanation. The better off you are, even when you are upset, the less angry you sound.

Keep in mind that your actions speak more loudly than your words, especially the words you use when you're upset. If you have mastery of your physical form, you will be able to communicate effectively while causing the least amount of harm to others.

A word of advice: Maintaining your distance from the situation is the best way to ensure your safety. When you find yourself becoming furious, try taking a step back. Because of the space between you, you will seem less threatening, and you will avoid any kind of physical confrontation. After all, you can always convey your point even if you're sitting at the other end of the table or in a different room.

Keep your focus on the here and now. This piece of advice is often given to married couples, but it is really incredibly useful for any form of relationship. Never, ever bring up old disagreements, regardless of whether or not you think you have a valid reason to do so. You're probably going to end yourself rehashing past debates and adding new points to the existing one you're in the middle of. Never go to the past for a solution to a problem in the here and now.

Above all else, safeguard the connection between you two. You need to make sure that you prioritise the relationships that are important to you, whether they be professional relationships with coworkers or personal relationships with friends or family members. You are going to have some conflicts with them, and they are going to do things that you are not going to enjoy, but despite this, they are still essential to you in some way or another. Just because you have a different opinion on one topic does not justify throwing everything aside. Most of the time, the things that might make you angry aren't important enough to warrant risking your connection with the people around you.

When things don't go as planned, they may quickly get nasty. However, they don't need to be much more unsightly than they already are, do they?

What Exactly Is The Meaning Of The Term "Anger Management"?

Anger management is a collection of abilities that may aid in spotting symptoms of anger and dealing with triggers in a constructive way. These skills can be helpful in reducing the negative effects of anger.

It requires a person to be able to recognise anger in its early stages and communicate their needs while maintaining their composure and being in control.

Managing anger does not include bottling it up or suppressing the feelings that accompany it. Instead, it requires acknowledging and accepting those feelings.

Anger management is a talent that can be learnt; given enough time, patience, and drive, almost anybody can figure out how to control their feelings and behaviours.

If anger is negatively affecting a relationship, especially if it is leading to violent or otherwise hazardous behaviour, a person may benefit from seeing a mental health professional or participating in a programme to manage anger if they feel that they need help controlling their anger.

There are, on the other hand, some quick tactics that you may try. There are some people who come to the realisation that they are able to handle these issues without the assistance of an expert.

Controlling one's anger

According to Mind, the ability to rein in one's rage may be split down into three distinct steps:

1. Be aware of the warning signs that indicate imminent anger.

2. Give yourself the space and time you need to investigate the triggers.

3. Employ strategies that will assist you in learning to control your anger.

=>Be aware of the warning signs that an outburst is about to occur.

In the heat of the moment, it might be difficult to maintain control of one's anger. On the other hand, it could be essential to recognise the emotion in its early stages. It has the potential to assist a person in reorienting their ideas in a more constructive manner.

The body will react in a physical way when anger is present. The release of the hormone adrenaline, sometimes known as the "fight-or-flight" hormone, helps to prepare a person for an encounter with a potentially dangerous situation.

The following are some possible consequences that might emerge from this:

- The sound of thumping pulses

- A faster rate of respiration

- A sensation of constriction that permeates the whole body

- Restlessness, foot-tapping, and pacing on the spot

- Jaws clenched and hands clenched tightly together

- Shuddering and profuse perspiration

It's possible that these physical manifestations point to a response that's proportionate to a given occurrence.

In any event, being aware of the symptoms at an early stage may be of use to a person in assessing whether or not the stimulus merits the physical response.

They may then make an attempt to regulate the physiological tension that they are experiencing if it is necessary.

less disagreements and uncertainties

Sometimes, we choose confrontation because we are motivated by hate for one another. Conflicts and debates emerge as a result of unique functions that differentiate how people are feeling in front of the various characters. In the event that you are familiar with the strategies used by the wonder the board, the occurrence of such circumstances may be reduced. One needs to be prepared to cope with differences in emotion even as outcomes rather than experiencing them as direct and expensive assaults. This will make one more resilient.

More effective communication

In most cases, shock is the result of erroneous perceptions, which may be rationally produced as a result of communication that has already been established between the persons who are being covered. In similar way, extraordinary social skills might be helpful in protecting an essential right method from astonishment or agitated circumstances. Having command of wonder and the ability to channel it in a productive manner will make communication a great deal less difficult and will give the impression that you are a person who is straightforward and easy to get along with.

Relationships that are both closer and more robust

Another advantage of using a wonder board is that it encourages you to inquire withinside the path of other people and makes it much easier for you to navigate nearby expensive and close-by businesses. When we lose control of a situation, our acquaintances and members of our immediate family are often the targets of our contempt. The ability to channel wonder will make us more suited for the use of an everyday life that is free from comparably horrific situations or changes of wonder.

When you pay attention to resolve on the side even as you are getting ready to manage marvel, you'll recognise when you are the reason at the back of any problem and when you aren't the purpose at the back of any hassle. You are going to be in a position to effortlessly control matters even though you aren't going to be penalised for doing so right even while the trouble is a right away end result of you. a magnificent work that is rather significant The treatment that your superiors provide you incorporates choosing the best technique to cope with generally recognised determination to your sentiments and along those lines the following path that they think you should take. The cycle presupposes that people are able to think rationally about a situation and be willing to take risks when necessary without shifting the burden of responsibility to another party.

Sincere condolences

To have sympathy for another person, you must first put yourself in their shoes and try to understand how they are seeing the world. Shock the board will instruct you on the ways to deal with differentiate, which is of incredible significance. Recognising contributes to a greater level of understanding and, as a result, less disputes. If you give yourself the opportunity to become aware of something, you will be able to see things from the point of view of other people, which will eliminate the potential for disputes. A significant portion of the time, shock may be avoided by preparing oneself in the style of method of an absence of understanding. The demonstration of compassion will improve as a result of teaching, which in turn will increase resourcefulness and gratitude for the opportunities that are collected. The effects of amazement are often replaced by ways of method of sympathetic understanding when individuals have the option to discover a state of affairs as consistent with each other's point of view. Shock the heads agencies are a form of remedy that is being prescribed more and more often these days, particularly for humans managing juveniles who are attempting to develop healthy social capabilities. These agencies are often provided in lieu of business as a result of a fostered hatred against the burden imposed by authority, or they are provided at home as a kind of accommodation. Shock the bosses' management implies that the instrument for generating revelry out of an approach to demand rate of your grief is present. Wonder is prompted by style of method of a lack of perception most of the time since the machine merges calming down and regulating the tendency throughout a profitable direction. The ability to coordinate will be of great assistance in the show of compassion, which will in turn promote persistence and appreciation for the opportunity collected. When one is presented with the opportunity to see a situation from the point of view of someone else, one's experience of awe may often be altered via the style of method of mindful appreciation.

The manner in which emotions are communicated is very personal. There has been a lot of study done on the issue of emotions, and researchers have come to the conclusion that all human beings feel these six basic emotions, although it is very subjective how they exhibit them.

It's not hard for any of us to empathise with these feelings at all. For instance, if you're waiting to hear the results of your test, you could find yourself experiencing a mixture of anxiety and excitement. It is difficult to single out just one feeling. The most obvious manifestation of an emotion to which individual responses are always going to be different is rage. It's possible that the depth and breadth of the rage you feel is not the same as what your sibling experiences. Emotions are felt in a unique way by each individual. It's quite natural to react to one emotion at a time, even if it's possible that two or more emotions might be present at the same moment.

The Reaction of the Physiological System

The way you feel might have a real effect on your body. If you suddenly get a knot in your gut, it might be an indication that you're experiencing nervous feelings. If you're anxious about anything, you could find that your hands start to sweat. Your body's involuntary reaction to a certain circumstance is controlled by your autonomic nervous system. This response is not something you can choose to do deliberately.

When you are feeling an emotion, your sympathetic nervous system is the part of your nervous system that governs the physiological reactions. The amygdala is the area of your brain that is responsible for the "flight or fight" reaction. This component of your system responds to that response. Anger has the most profound effect on one particular organ known as the amygdala.

The Reaction in Terms of Behaviour

Your behaviour is the culmination of the process that begins when you convey how you are feeling emotionally. A great number of ways of expressing feelings are shared globally. For instance, a frown may signal that someone is furious, while a grin can show that someone is joyful. Both of these facial expressions can be used interchangeably.

It's natural for humans to infer meaning from the facial expressions and body language of others around them. However, being really aware of our own feelings as well as those of others is a quality that only a small percentage of individuals have. Emotional awareness refers to this state of being. It is really necessary to be conscious of your feelings in order to have an effective method of dealing with them. Emotional awareness is being able to recognise, accept, and appreciate your own emotions without making value judgements about them.

Why are it so important to have emotions?

When it comes to comprehending your feelings, the components described before are of the utmost importance. As we've seen, our feelings not only influence the choices that we make but also play a role in determining how motivated we are to perform a certain job. The following are some of the many reasons why emotional states are so important to how you think and act.

They give you the ability to do something about it.

Taking action is the most important step you need to take in order to achieve anything in life. When it comes to doing effectively in terms of taking action, your emotional reactions help you to do so. For example, if you have a significant job interview, your feelings may cause you to feel worried and frightened about the experience. As a result of this, you may decide to devote extra time to prepare so that you can provide a good performance during the job interview. You were inspired to take action as a result of experiencing these feelings, which led to your success. In a wide variety of different contexts, we often engage in certain behaviours with the expectation of generating favourable outcomes.

They assist us in recognising potential dangers.

Emotions have the ability to guide us away from potentially harmful circumstances. Darwin was the one who first proposed the process of natural selection, and one component of this idea is that a living thing's chances of survival improve in proportion to the degree to which it is adaptable to the emotions it experiences. When we feel threatened by anything, our natural inclination is to run away as quickly as possible in order to alleviate the anxiety that we are experiencing.

Managing Anger In The Presence Of Complete Strangers

It is not simple to vent your rage on a person you have never met. To begin, you are not familiar with his character, and he is not familiar with yours. Second, there is a possibility that you may be misinterpreted. There have been a few reports of weird individuals acting violently to vent their fury, and those reports have been told. This might lead to a run-in with the law or a civil lawsuit being brought before a judge. Because they do not care about how you are feeling, it is possible that you will be unable to have a productive conversation with them.

In situations like this, you have the following choices:

Ignore the unknown person.

Ignore a strange person who continues bothering you if you find yourself becoming irritated by the situation. He is not worth the effort that you put into dealing with him.

Get out of here!

Get away from him if he persists in doing whatever it is that's driving you crazy. Why put up with his behaviour if you have the option to leave? Under such conditions, it is the most viable alternative for you to consider.

Have a conversation with the newcomer.

You may try to reason with the stranger if he appears to have a level head, and you can urge him to stop doing whatever it is that's bothering you by saying that you find it bothersome.

Make a call to the authorities.

It is already considered a public disturbance if he does not listen to you and continues to irritate you and the other people in the area where he is. You are free to contact the police. But you really should save this option for last. Spending time with the police is probably not something you want to do. Try to keep your cool and keep your temper under control as much as you can. Being the target of another person's rage will get you nowhere, and it will do the same for them.

In spite of the fact that you often caution your children not to engage in conversation with strangers, you recently did so. You have responded to the acts taken by the stranger. Therefore, it is important to keep in mind that you should act rather than react to the situation.

It goes without saying that there are always going to be exceptions to the norm, such as the time you saw a wounded guy pass out. You have no compassion if you choose to ignore his pleas for assistance. The most prudent thing to do in this circumstance is to call an ambulance. When deciding what course of action to take, use your good judgement.

You May Trace Each Of These Things Back To The Origin Of Your Anger... Take Good Care Of Them To Prevent Them From Throwing It Away.

Earlier, in the chapter before this one, we discussed what we called the "anger tree." What really prompts your furious responses is what's at the bottom of this whole mess. It's possible that while you're in the thick of things, you don't even realise what it is that's driving you crazy; all you can see is yourself completely losing it. However, getting to the bottom of those underlying emotions and the causes that lie behind them may make a world of difference.

There's a good reason why the manner in which your children carry themselves and the things they do set off an emotional response in you. There is a justification behind it. And it is on these topics that we are going to go into more depth right now.

There are four things that contribute to your anger:

1.) Your Expectations That Were Not Met:

Every single parent's goal should be to bring up a responsible child. One aspect of this is that we want children to have a positive demeanour and outlook on life. These are the requirements and standards that we impose on them. In addition to having these expectations, we make a concerted effort to instill the practises that will enable them to demonstrate the sort of conduct that we anticipate from them. It is not a coincidence that our tempers flare whenever they do anything that is not in line with our expectations.

One of the reasons we become upset with our children is because we have unmet expectations. The fact that they didn't complete their tasks when you wanted them to, or that they didn't get the grade you wanted them to get in school, or that they spoke to a stranger in a way that you didn't raise them to do are just some of the things that may make you furious. There are many more things, however, that could make you upset.

When you find yourself becoming angry with your children, bring your focus within and ask yourself why this is happening. It's possible that you were let down or disappointed by them, and that's the problem.

2.) Having a Personal Attitude Towards Their Behaviour:

Children will always behave like children. The sooner you acknowledge and come to terms with this fact, the more easily you will be able to deal with the mess that they have created.

There are behaviours that your children now engage in that are perfectly normal at this stage in their development. These behaviours include having an angry outburst, starting conflicts with their friends, being mopey when their needs are not satisfied, and even sometimes being obstinate.

There is a good chance that none of these things are done on purpose to spite you or to minimise the efforts you make as their parent to teach them to be responsible children. It's simply that they are behaving like kids! The majority of the time, a parent's anger is caused by the mistaken belief that their child is acting intentionally in order to provoke the parent's reaction. On the other hand, this is not always the case.

When you finally come to terms with the fact that you shouldn't take other people's acts so personally, you'll be able to start letting go of some of your resentment and reacting to their conduct with less aggravation and more empathy.

You will also have a far greater chance of coming up with much more effective techniques and inventive solutions to deal with their behaviours.

For instance, if you know that a typical 7-year-old is hyperactive and often fidgety, you could find that it is difficult for that youngster to remain seated for a lengthy meal with the rest of the family. Therefore, if after twenty-five minutes of eating together, he begins to provoke a conflict with one of his siblings. You may choose not to scold at him for creating a fight at the table by understanding that this behaviour is a natural part of being

7 years old. Instead, you can have him get up and refill water cups to give him something else to put his energy onto.

3.) Emotions That Aren't Dealt With:

As parents, there are instances when the reasons for our furious outbursts have nothing to do with the conduct of our children. Their activities may serve as the catalyst, but they are in no way the primary cause.

Take into consideration the following: You may have had a stressful day at work, received a reprimand from your supervisor at the workplace, or gotten into an altercation with a client or a coworker. You're already carrying around the baggage of unresolved feelings that you repressed at the moment and haven't dealt with yet. Then, when you arrive home, your child does something that should never get on your nerves or warrant an outburst from you, but boom! I'll see you later.

The suppressed, bad feelings that you carried home with you are the source of the anger that you display at that time. It is not always the result of what the kid did.

When you are able to be more in touch with your feelings, you will have a stronger ability to keep those feelings under control when anything sets them off.

4.) Stress on the Body, the Mind, the Bank Account, and the Emotions:

The majority of parents put in long hours at work each week in order to provide a nice life for their children. And it's possible that juggling all of their jobs and obligations will be challenging for them.

When you have an excessive amount of work to do, you want everything to go off without a hitch so that you may complete each task as quickly as possible and move on to the next item. This situation puts you under a certain amount of stress, which might manifest in your body, mind, or both.

When you find yourself in a circumstance like this one, it is important to be conscious that stress is probably the root cause of your short temper with your kid rather than the action that he has taken.

Reduce the amount of work you have to do and find a way to strike a healthy balance in your life so that you can effectively manage all of the duties that come with being a parent.

Make an effort to be more organised, make a plan for the next day the night before, prepare meals in bulk, and get up earlier. Simply put, you should do whatever it takes to become more effective and to take charge of your day. This will assist you in lowering your stress levels and the negative impact stress has on your body, mind, and emotions.

In terms of finances, you have the option of deciding to find a job that pays more, working more hours, or starting a side company in order to raise your income and put yourself in a better position financially.

Sign Up For A Class On Managing Your Angry Moods.

People who struggle with anger disorders may enrol in anger management programmes at a large number of community assistance centres and mental health clinics around the country. Classes on how to control one's anger may last anywhere from a single evening to an entire weekend or even a number of consecutive weeks. There are lessons that you can sign up for at a minimal fee, and there are other classes that you can attend without having to pay anything at all. In anger management programmes, the primary emphasis is on assisting you in locating the specific cause of your outbursts of rage, and you will also be provided with opportunities to learn beneficial skills and methods for managing your anger. Lessons on how to control one's anger often focus more on knowledge and theory than on actual application. Have a conversation with your therapist about anger management programmes in your area, or sign up for one of these programmes online.

Managing Conflict with Irate Individuals

You are not someone who struggles with anger, but you know at least one or two other people who do. Therefore, it is imperative that you acquire the skills necessary to cope with angry individuals. Dealing with angry individuals requires a significant amount of patience and composure since it makes it easier for you to get furious yourself. You need to have emotional intelligence if you want to interact with someone who has problems controlling their rage. Being emotionally intelligent enables you to take command of your own emotions and keep them under control, all the while keeping in mind that other people aren't as fortunate as you are to have the wisdom to keep their own feelings under control. Try the following method when interacting with a person who has problems controlling their anger:

1. Keep your cool like a glacier: Dealing with an angry individual demands you to maintain a level head and not allow your own emotions get the best of you while the other person is expressing their own. Maintaining your composure demonstrates that you are attentive to what the other person is saying and letting out. Make it clear to the other person that you are really interested in learning more about the issue at hand. Never respond angrily to someone else's anger. However, while interacting with an angry individual, you should not allow yourself to be manipulated by the rage of the other person.

2. Keep in mind that you are interacting with a person: people have varying responses to the same set of circumstances, and our behaviours also vary from one another. When interacting with a person who has problems controlling their anger, it is important to treat that person on an individual basis. Make an effort to empathise with him and comprehend his position from his perspective. Put yourself in his position so that you may fully comprehend what he is going through.

3. Keep a good attitude: Instead of merely acting, show that you are willing to listen to the other person and that you are going to do something constructive to settle the problem. Simply because you are taking someone seriously does not imply that you will give in to their demands; all it means is that you are taking them seriously. When you have someone beneath you who is upset, you

should not try to calm them down by quoting laws or regulations for them since it will not be effective. It is perhaps possible that it will make the situation much worse overall. Before you can scold the individual or have a conversation with them about their behaviour, you need to give them some time to compose themselves first.

4. Take it Behind Closed Doors: Do not allow a conflict to escalate in public. Find a private place to speak to the person since this will enable you to discuss things in the appropriate manner, and the person's anger could even calm up a little before you arrive to the place where you will be talking things with them.

5. Be wary of persons who don't show their rage: There are certain individuals who don't make their anger known. Be on the lookout for any indication that

these individuals are becoming agitated at any given moment. Be on the lookout for warning indications such as pouting, being silent even while in the presence of others, avoiding certain topics, or refusing to take action and engage. If a person exhibits any of these behaviours, it is safe to assume that they are harbouring some level of suppressed rage.

Having to interact with irate individuals has the potential to deplete even your reserves of patience and composure, but you really must find a way to maintain your composure at all times.

What Kind Of Experience Should You Have When Visiting A Professional Counselor Or Medical Doctor?

If your professional therapist believes that it is essential, they will refer you to a medical doctor or psychiatrist so that they can make an accurate diagnosis of any underlying emotional, physical, or mental health concerns that may be the cause of your anger problems.

This is accomplished by a battery of examinations, the specifics of which will vary according to the condition the physician is looking for as well as the age of the patient. Children who have problems controlling their anger may be subjected to a battery of examinations during which they are required to look at images, colour, choose blocks from a moving table, and participate in other activities designed to determine whether or not they have attention deficit hyperactivity disorder (ADHD), attention deficit hyperactivity disorder (ADD), and other similar conditions. Tests will be administered to adults according to their age group and what the doctor may believe is the reason based on the symptoms given by either the patient, the therapist, or both the patient and the therapist. It is possible that a series of X-rays and CT scans will be performed in order to look for any injuries, lesions, or other abnormalities.

Depending on the results of these tests, the physician may suggest that more medical treatment may be necessary, as well as prescribe a variety of medications, such as an antidepressant, anxiety medication, or medicine to stabilise the patient's mood. Counselling for anger control may be all that is suggested instead.

Unless they have reason to believe that the patient is experiencing significant levels of stress or anxiety that might be harmful to their physical health, most doctors prefer not to give medication to their patients for anger management. Not only do most of these medicines come with unpleasant side effects including a horrible thirst, headaches, nausea, and tremors, but they also have the potential to become addicted, which may make the problem of anger control much worse. They have the ability to change a person's state of mind as well. People who have problems controlling their anger already struggle with a state of mind that is disturbed and a lack of control.

Before turning to medicine, a doctor will always suggest speaking with a counsellor or visiting a wellness centre, unless they have reason to believe the individual poses a threat to themselves or others.

There are assessments that individuals may complete online to determine whether or not they have an underlying problem that is the root cause of their irritability and mood swings; however, these assessments are only a suggestion, and they truly should not be considered as a diagnosis. If you have the impression that your anger is just the tip of the iceberg, it is in your best interest to seek the guidance of a trained counsellor or a qualified medical expert.

If you have attempted therapy, but feel that your problems are becoming worse, you should go to your primary care physician again for guidance. It's possible that you need a new kind of counselling, or that they need to do some further tests. The important thing is not to quit up even if it seems like you are not making any progress since it takes time to build things up and much longer to tear them down.

The Fourth Chapter: Remain Calm

The majority of individuals experience feelings of anger and frustration because they are unable to learn how to relax. They are already so occupied with their responsibilities that they have forgotten how to slow down a little bit.

Angry outbursts are frequently the result of a buildup of stressors and anxieties that is greater than the individual's ability to cope with and alleviate those stresses and worries.

There are moments when you feel as like you are going to blow your top, and you have lost the ability to manage the tension and fury that you are experiencing.

When this occurs, the best way to cope with these suppressed feelings is to take the third step in anger management, which is to remain calm.

There are a lot of different activities that might help you relax and calm down when you're feeling tense or angry. When you feel as if your anger is rising out of your control, you may attempt any one of the following techniques:

1. Take a few long, slow breaths.

You may get control of your wrath by doing this, which despite its seeming simplicity is really one of the most powerful methods. In addition to supplying you with the oxygen that your body need, it enables you to reflect on the situation at hand and offers you the opportunity to do so.

When you are confronted with a stressful situation, it is important to take a moment to pause and focus on your breathing even if it is just for a few seconds at a time. In what ways does it help you to control your emotions?

First, a moment of focused attention may be gained by taking a few full breaths. When you're feeling angry, shifting your attention to the rise and fall of your chest while you breathe deeply will help you transition your focus from that anger to the peace that comes with deep breathing.

Second, taking a few slow, deep breaths might make it easier to think more clearly. Inhaling deeply encourages the entrance of oxygen into your lungs, which is necessary for the performance of a variety of functions throughout the body.

Oxygen has a number of responsibilities in the body, one of which is to provide cells with the energy they require to carry out their duties.

Oxygen is absolutely necessary for the survival of the neurons and other cells in your brain, the most important of which is thought. The more oxygen that is supplied to the brain, the greater your capacity for clear thinking will be.

2. Devote some of your time to your own needs.

This is something that a lot of individuals often overlook doing. They are so focused on completing the duties that they have been given that they forget to eat in a healthy manner, get some exercise, or even take a break from their packed schedule.

Spending some time on your own does not need you to take a whole day off during your hectic week; even just a few minutes will suffice as long as you are able to keep your mind off of the things that are stressing you out and worrying you.

There are several activities that you may do in order to give yourself some time to relax and recharge. To unwind while you are at the workplace, take advantage of the thirty minutes allotted for coffee breaks and go for a stroll instead.

When there are deadlines that need to be met, the majority of individuals experience feelings of stress.

As you stroll slowly outside of your office building, do your best to forget about the approaching deadlines. Take in the sights of the people walking by, take note of the recently opened businesses in the area, and observe the birds flying in the sky.

You may also attempt to sneak in some time to read your favourite book or listen to some music that will calm you down. This is another option.

What Exactly Is The Concept Of Parenting Triggers?

It is useful to see parenting triggers within the larger context of your life while we are discussing them. To put it another way, you are not the cause of your own anger. It is necessary for something to take place before you may lose your anger. This idea is summed up rather clearly in a study that was conducted in 2018, and it states that "certain stressors, deriving from parental or child situational or contextual domains influence parenting stress, which also accompanies difficulties in adjusting to the parenting role."31 This quotation has a lot of information that needs to be analysed.

First, the researchers discuss the many sources of stress. As a consequence of this, you do not get irritated by yourself.

You don't simply explode in anger at the drop of a hat, even if you're coping with some serious underlying emotional concerns (like the death of a loved one, for example). There must be a trigger for everything to start happening.

Second, these sources of stress may be broken down into three categories: the parent, the kid, and the setting. This phrase indicates that any one of these factors, or all three of them together, has the potential to affect your response, which may then lead to the beginning of rage. In the worst possible scenario, you will be assaulted by all three of them.

The third source of stress in parenting is having trouble adapting to one's new position as a parent. This does not imply that you won't be able to adapt to your new role as a parent. It suggests that moving from one setting to another might make it challenging to return to the position of a parent. Don't be concerned. This kind of thing takes place on a regular basis. Take for instance the fact that you are a very busy professional in the workplace. When you go through the door of your house, you take off your hat as a working woman and put on the hat of a mother. Because of this abrupt change in mentality, it may be difficult for us parents to readjust to our new roles as parents.

As you can see, we are subjected to a variety of stresses during the course of the day. Therefore, it is necessary for us to have an understanding of how our responses and how we concentrate on the environment around us are affected by the various stresses. Because we have previously covered the topic of environmental factors (such as the weather, traffic, and job), we will restrict our attention to the impacts exerted by parents and children.

Recognising Our Responses to Events

In her book published in 2006 titled Raising Our Children, Raising Ourselves: Transforming parent-child interactions from reaction and struggle to freedom, power, and pleasure, Naomi Aldort makes an interesting point about how we as parents respond to the actions of our children. She contends that parents do not always behave in accordance with the facial expressions of their children. Our responses, on the other hand, are founded on the challenges we encounter while attempting to analyse our own feelings.

Consider the following:

The reason we respond the way we do when our children scream, moan, or throw tantrums is not always because of the behaviour of our children. Instead, our dissatisfaction may stem from the fact that we are unable to fathom the reasons why our children behave the way that they do.

The aha moment has finally arrived. This moment:

Children do not have the psychological development necessary to properly handle the feelings that they experience. On the other hand, as adults, we have the capacity to comprehend our sentiments and to work through them in a manner that is as constructive as possible.

Are you getting the gist of what I'm trying to say here?

Because we are unable to properly process our own feelings, we are often the source of our own dissatisfaction, as well as rage and even disappointment. As a result, we need to acquire a grasp on our own sentiments before we can properly manage the expressions that our children display. For this understanding, some introspection is required.

I'd want to do this workout beside you if that's okay.

Consider the most recent incident in which you were furious with your kid.

Think back to what took place and how your kid responded to it.

From that point on, consider how you were feeling. Consider how the response of your kid made you feel at that moment. Were you in a bad mood? Sad? Are you upset? Are you dismayed?

Now, think about the reasons why you had that feeling. Be truthful and sincere with yourself. Whom did you have in mind when you spoke those things, your kid, or yourself?

After you've had some time to process the situation and think about what went wrong, it's important to consider how things might have been handled better. There is a considerable probability that you may come up with a number of alternative approaches to dealing with the circumstance.

Make a commitment to yourself as the last step. Make a promise to yourself that, going forward, you will actively work to approach situations in a different manner.

You need to give this exercise of reflection a lot of thought if you want to get the most out of it. This is the kind of workout that will always help you gain a feel of how you are dealing with the things that are going on around you.

What Exactly Are The Issues With Controlling One's Anger?

We are going to have to come to terms with the truth that we are prone to feelings of rage and irritation from time to time. Because of this, we may be considered natural humans. It is possible for us to vent our anger via the use of violence in a variety of contexts, including but not limited to the following: when there is a dispute between us because we have different beliefs; when someone criticises our character; when we are deceived or mistreated; and so on. In these kinds of circumstances, anger has the potential to become a problem that calls for treatment and assistance in order to prevent it from causing damage to either the people around us or to ourselves.

It's possible that the harmful repercussions of rage aren't restricted to only acts of physical hostility. This is due to the fact that such harmful impacts may also result from our own internal bad ideas of violence, which may not really be violent but nonetheless have an effect on both our physical and emotional well-being. When we are angry, the things that we say or do may have repercussions not just at home but also at work, particularly on the connections that we have with other people.

Your capacity to pay attention is typically what determines how you act when you are furious, and ultimately, it is what regulates the feelings of anger and frustration that you experience each time you feel yourself rising up. In this light, it is of the utmost importance for us to keep an eye out for any problems with controlling our anger that we may represent or people around us who could be experiencing emotions of rage. These are the following:

Abusive language and aggressive behaviour

This involves actions such as screaming, using harsh words, or cussing out others. Some individuals may even threaten the people around them when they are physically abusing others by hurling things or being aggressive towards them. These are only a few instances of aggressiveness that comes from the outside.

Anger that arises from inside

It manifests itself in a manner that is more subtly indicative of the negative effects associated with rage. This may include redirecting feelings of anger and irritation inside rather than displaying them directly to the people around you or to those who have caused you harm. One example of this would be saying "I'm not going to let you win." This significantly raises the possibility that the anger will transform into self-hatred, and it also increases the likelihood that you will withdraw from your family and friends. There is also the possibility that the person may hurt themselves or possibly end their own life.

Aggression that does not involve physical conflict.

Although this kind of anger management issue may not be as severe as the other two types of anger management difficulties described above, the fact remains that passive rage may have serious repercussions for the relationships in your life. This kind of rage might be shown passively by avoiding eye contact with other people, not engaging in conversation with them, or wilfully shirking responsibilities at home or at work that have been delegated to you. Because of behaviours like these, you run the risk of causing harm to your relationships as well as to the individuals in your immediate environment, including yourself.

Bear in mind that showing your anger to other people may seriously damage both you and the relationships you have with the other people in your environment. When it comes to matters involving children, this is an exceptionally risky course of action. Short-term and long-term impacts are caused as a result of the immediate mental and physical difficulties that are caused by this. Short-term repercussions include job loss and troubles with the police, while long-term effects have the potential to produce mental and bodily damage. Even though you may not have physically acted aggressively or even raised your voice, you may be able to recognise these behaviours when they are shown by others. This indicates that once you have an understanding of them, you need to make sure that you address them in order to lessen the influence that they have on the lives of individuals and on their general well-being.

Here Are Ten Suggestions That Will Help Bring Peace and Harmony to Your Relationship

Now, let's get down to the nitty-gritty of the situation. Your connection with yourself is the place to start if you want to bring more calm and harmony into the relationships in your life.

Everything starts with YOU, your thinking, and both what you want out of the relationship for yourself and what you are prepared to offer to the other person in the relationship.

It is necessary for you to be truthful, open, and transparent with the thinking patterns and limiting beliefs that may prevent you from genuinely opening up to the possibility of a beautiful and satisfying connection with another person.

You have to be honest with yourself, your views, and your objectives, and you have to keep your attention on the things that you can really contribute to the discussion. Keeping in mind that whatever you bring will cause a response, and that this reaction is exactly what you meant to acquire in the first place. Keeping in mind that anything you bring will cause a reaction.

Consider it in this way: you get what you give, and you are what you give. Think about it that way. The principle of Murphy's law. When people believe that they are receiving love in return from another person, they are far more likely to freely offer their love to that person. I use the term 'love' in a generic sense to refer to the components that combine to produce that emotion.

The following are some practises that will assist you in becoming better at establishing greater internal and external peace, harmony, and connectedness in your relationships and with yourself.

How To Stay Away From Tantrums

Being aware of and prepared for your baby's need is essential if you want to prevent temper tantrums. Once again, this is not a simple task, and if Mom or Dad is already worn out and irritated, it becomes much more challenging. The period of time spent sleeping, eating, napping, and getting ready for bed should, to the greatest extent feasible, all adhere to the same pattern. The familiarity of this routine instills in young children a feeling of safety and security, which has a very soothing effect. Aim to prepare ahead of time on days when you are aware that the routine may vary (grandma and grandpa, despite their best efforts, are infamous disruptors).

This consistency may serve as an additional incentive for good behaviour or as a springboard for an unplanned sleep if a baby is being irritable. It should come as no surprise that there is no failsafe approach that can guarantee flawless behaviour at all times. You can very much count on having to deal with a temper tantrum at some point in time. Uncannily, children have a propensity to have their most boisterous temper tantrums in the midst of upscale public places like grocery stores and restaurants.

An additional point to bear in mind is that an older kid should not resort to temper tantrums or other forms of disobedient behaviour in order to acquire what they want. If you give in and purchase the item to silence the child's cries, however, the child's behaviour will simply become more defiant.If you believe that your baby's tantrums are becoming more frequent and out of control, or if it takes a significant amount of time to calm them down, you should make an appointment with your baby's paediatrician to rule out the possibility of a more severe health issue.In addition, your frame of mind will determine the manner in which you respond. Create development plans for your kid that are both realistic and exciting. Maintain a high level of vigilance on your infant while they are in an unfamiliar environment or with new people. Because your child is still developing new skills and might be easily frustrated, it is important to spend time interacting with them.

It is a natural developmental stage that all children will go through at some point, and it won't continue forever (although if at times it may feel as though it would never stop). Maintaining your composure and demonstrating to your child that you are attentive to their requirements can help you get through the years of temper tantrums with ease.

When Should You Start To Be Worried?

It is crucial to see a mental health expert if you observe that your child is having difficulty coping with their rage or if the tantrums continue for lengthy periods of time. As you and your toddler work through these feelings together, a therapist may be able to provide particular direction and support to both of you throughout this process.

▷ The one who acts irrationally most of the time.

"Give it to me in that green cup!"

"I don't want to go to bed now!" you exclaim.

"I don't want to put trousers on today!"

Does this sound familiar? Why even bring this up as a point of contention?

You are the parent, therefore it seems sense for you to be the one who establishes the ground rules, right?

I'm willing to wager that your kid has a different opinion.

Toddlers are in the developmental period when they are becoming more conscious of their feelings, testing the boundaries of their independence, and exploring their independence. Because of this, they have a strong desire to make their own choices.

As a result, in order to demonstrate their capabilities, they have decided to make choices that seem to be diametrically opposed to yours. Even though you may perceive this to be unreasonable, it is quite reasonable.

When it comes to the various factors that have an effect on the behaviour of a kid, the child's own feelings are at the very centre. At about four or five years of age, the portion of the brain that is responsible for reasoning and self-regulation starts to mature. As a result, toddlers are motivated by their feelings, namely what it is that they desire, rather than what we think would be best for them.

Consider this time a chance to teach your kid healthy coping behaviours that they may use in the future. You, as a parent, have options on how to respond to the illogical actions of your kid, including the following:

Exhibit some empathy. You don't want to be one of those parents who ignores their children whenever they make a request because you don't want to set a bad example. The ability to make free choices is a blessing that is innate to every person. Everyone, including your kid, makes their own choices about what they want. You want to indicate that you understand the point your kid is trying to make and that you are on their side, even if it may not be the greatest decision for the time in your view. Despite this, you want to show that you are on their team. For instance, if you are having problems persuading your child to go to bed, you may try telling them something along the lines of, "I know you don't want to go to bed now, but if you don't, you will wake up late and miss out on having fun with mum just before school tomorrow."

Take charge of the situation. Getting into a power struggle with your kid is the worst thing that you could possibly do to them. Maintain your composure just as you would if your kid were having a temper tantrum. Keep a level head. A parent who is sad in comparison to their kid who is distressed is the ideal recipe for guilt.

Give your youngster the opportunity to make their own decisions. Place a few alternatives in front of your youngster, and then wait for him or her to choose one. This provides your kid with a feeling of control and offers them the opportunity to make their own choices within the parameters you provide for them. For instance, you may inquire as to whether or not the individual would like to put on the green or the blue clothing. alternatively, "Would you like a banana or an apple for a snack?" You might provide your young child with a third alternative if he or she is having problems settling on a choice. Keep in mind that toddlers experience both a feeling of control and success when they are able to make their own decisions within the boundaries that you establish for them. This strategy may be used by parents to prevent power disputes and to assist their toddlers in developing a feeling of control and achievement on their own.

The Sources of Your Irritability, Chapter Three

If you want to teach your kid how to control his anger, the first thing you need to do is assist him recognise the things that set him off and get him worked up. You will be able to avoid any conditions that may cause your kid to get angry and, as a result, prevent any furious outbursts if you are able to recognise the triggers.

You are able to assist your kid in recognising the events that provoke anger in him.

When your kid is able to recognise circumstances of this kind, he will be in a better position to analyse the factors that are contributing to the negative feelings that he is now experiencing.

In addition to this, it will help your kid understand his emotions, which will make it much simpler for him to deal with them.

Instead of your youngster suffering a full-blown meltdown, corrective action may be performed quickly.

You are undoubtedly aware of the many circumstances or reasons that might set off your child's behavioural issues. However, the purpose of this part is to assist your kid in comprehending and recognising the triggers that affect him. When he finally understands what sets him off, then and only then will he be able to control his rage.

It is not difficult to describe what a trigger is to an adult in any way. Nevertheless, how can you describe what a trigger is to your child? Telling your kid that everything that generates a response is considered a trigger is a straightforward explanation that you may use with them. To provide one specific example, tickling is a great way to induce laughter. Now that you know what a trigger is, you may tease your young one, and as soon as he begins giggling, he will realise what it implies. After you have finished tickling him, you should tell him that the laughter he was experiencing was caused by your tickling. After that, you may proceed to describe what we mean when we talk about rage triggers.

An action, emotion, setting, or pretty much anything else that causes your kid to get angry may be referred to as an anger trigger. Why is it so crucial to recognise the factors that cause one to get angry? If you are able to identify the triggers, you will be able to assist your child in avoiding similar circumstances, learning strategies to deal with his feelings, or all of these things.

When it comes to children, some of the most prevalent causes of anger include things like worry, hunger, exhaustion, irritation, and a feeling of unfairness; however, these are not the only things that may provoke anger in children.

3. Reacting to agitated sensations of anger

After considering the effects that frequency and intensity have on anger, the next step is to think about how anger is handled. When individuals are furious, they often either excessively express it, suppress it, or try to calm it down within.

Learn more about each common method of anger management by looking at the examples provided.

Excessively express

When a person's anger is inappropriately conveyed, it is easy to see and comprehend that the individual is furious.

They might rant, say things that are harsh and improper, become physically aggressive, and even get violent.

Put down

When a person suppresses their anger, it may be impossible to tell that they are furious. However, repressed anger is almost always displayed in a passive-aggressive manner, even though it is never explicitly articulated as rage.

The inability to cooperate, carelessness, and missed deadlines are all potential side effects of bottling up your emotions.

Sometimes suppressed rage may surface in the form of a spontaneous outburst directed against a target that was neither planned nor suitable.

Try to keep a level head.

Some individuals are able to learn how to control their anger on the inside, without ever having to resort to direct or indirect expression of it. When people have learnt to control their anger in this manner, you won't be able to tell when they are furious anymore. They also refrain from taking revenge in ways that might be harmful to their colleagues or the environment of the workplace.

What Is It?

Either venting all of your frustrations at once or bottling it up within might result in unfavourable consequences. And although if settling your anger on the inside won't have the same adverse effects as these other reactions, it still won't take advantage of the opportunities presented by the fact that you're angry.

Which of the following do you believe to be a beneficial consequence of anger?

Alternate Meanings:

1. It contributes to the enhancement of relationships.

2. It motivates you to seek retribution.

3. It gives you more influence and control over other people

A response

Your connections with other people may improve as a result of your anger. It may assist you with expressing your viewpoint, which is something that other people would probably appreciate if you do so. On the other hand, anger that results in vengeance or that is channelled into making threats or demonstrating your dominance over others is likely to have unfavourable repercussions.

Affect and State of Mind

Our emotions serve as a driving force behind our behaviours. They alert us whenever we are in danger, which is why they are so important to our ability to live. Danger in today's civilization is much different from what it was 10,000 years ago, when we lived in primitive dwellings that left us vulnerable to the weather, when we had to hunt for our food, harvest our flora, and face deadly animals that wanted to eat us, and when we were exposed to these dangers because we lived in an open environment.

Even if there are less threats to our immediate existence in the contemporary world, our brains are still in the process of adjusting to the new era. We continue to be driven by the same instincts as our ancient ancestors, who battled the weather on a daily basis as they fought for their physical lives to be preserved.

Their instincts drove them to search for food and water, and when they were confronted with a hazardous beast, they either fled or fought. These feelings are still necessary in modern life since they warn us of potentially dangerous circumstances, get us ready for action, and assist us in making choices; yet, we tend to rely on them too often.

The incessant feeling that is mood is an emotion that just won't go away. Even if the situation that triggered the emotions is long behind us, the negative sentiments continue to linger, and it may be tough to rid ourselves of them. This is harmful because feelings should only go a short distance and stop when the threat is no longer there. They should not run an exhausting marathon that brings everyone else along for the ride.

There are six phases that an emotion goes through as it moves through its life cycle, and they are as follows:

Activation refers to the process through which our brains bring about a reaction to a stimulus.

Modulation is the process through which we decide how to react as well as the amount of intensity of that response.

The time of preparation has arrived, and at this point, your brain is quite busy. It is a matter of negotiating the release of hormones, and in the case of anger, your heart rate rises along with your blood pressure in order to give your arms and legs with a heavier blood supply so that you can respond fast to a physical attack. This is done so that you can defend yourself against a physical assault. Your digestive system stops working, and your lungs expand so that they can take in more oxygen.

Once an emotion has taken hold of you, you have very little influence over the way in which your body prepares you for it, but you do have some control over how you react to it. It does not matter how you choose to react, whether with temperance or wrath; either way, what you do counts as an action.

Feedback: Feelings continue to exist even after an action has been taken. Your thoughts offered you feedback as to whether the activity was beneficial or not. It is never productive to be enraged over anything. After giving it some thought, your aggressive behaviour may get you what you want in the here and now, but it is not a long-term solution. In the end, you end up losing everything.

Deactivation: At some point in time, the feeling passes, and you go on with the rest of your life. People who are filled with wrath find it difficult to detach themselves from the feeling, and as they go through the world, they bring a negative disposition with them like a cloud that follows them.

You are attempting to get to a point in which you are better able to manage furious feelings by using the strategies that are presented in this book. We want to guide you to the "sweet spot," which is a location between complacency and wrath. There is a point where you should land, and we want to bring you there. As your brain receives the emotional information and you go through the six phases, the following are examples of anger that have been inadequately managed:

Unhealthy Activation During the activation stage, a severe malfunction known as hypersensitivity manifests itself in those who are prone to outbursts of rage and other emotions. You start looking for triggers that will set off your anger rather than waiting for genuine impulses to gauge how things will play out in your head. In addition, even our so-called "real" impulses are so finely calibrated that they pose a significant threat to the mental and emotional health of the individual.

Unhealthy Modulation People who are naturally aggressive have a tendency to overreact when they feel upset because they are hypersensitive to anger and they are unable to self-regulate and moderate their impulses. This causes them to behave out in ways that are unhealthy for themselves and others around them. Because of this, people develop violent habits, which they then need to intentionally work to break via the use of practise.

Unhealthy Preparation: If you are hypersensitive to furious feelings, and that parlays into an overreaction during the modulation stage, then it is likely that you will walk into situations without properly preparing yourself. It becomes more difficult to go through your alternatives when they are shrouded in fog, which makes it more difficult to make a decision. In addition, the emotional centres are in such a basic and instinctual condition that the frontal lobes have a hard time executing their will upon the self to make an acceptable option that is proportionate to the occurrence that is producing the anger. This is because the frontal lobes are trying to execute their will upon the self to make an appropriate response to the occurrence that is creating the anger. Instead, the emotional centres are making hasty, and ultimately regrettable, preparations for whatever is to come.

Unhealthy response: People who are hypersensitive to anger are now in a poor spot, since the illogical response that has been planned is to attack the object that generated the anger. This action is unhealthy because it is an assault on the source of the anger. There is no hope that a suitable response will be available, and it is quite probable that the strong reaction will not even get through to the intended recipient.

Unhealthy feedback: persons who are aggressive believe that their acts are justified since their thinking has become twisted and is no longer sensible. The conclusion they reached from their analysis is that the victim deserved what happened to them, and because they did not provide an adequate or truthful assessment, the pattern would likely continue.

Unhealthy Deactivation: Angry feelings that do not deactivate at a proper moment and continue to linger become a person's mood, which badly impacts everyone around the brooding angry individual who cannot come down from his or her furious position. This kind of deactivation is known as "unhealthy deactivation." Even when the mood phase has passed, anger may linger on as a sense of resentment, which is constantly there and always inflicting pain on the person who harbours it. There is never any resolution to any issue, and the emotional cycle is never really finished. Neither of these things can ever be said to be true.

Parenting that lacks consistency

Your kid may be said to have inconsistent parenting if, during his or her childhood, the youngster is cared for by a variety of different people. Your kid may have problems with anger management as a result of the several carers since they all have different expectations and the repercussions are unexpected.

The youngster goes through life never knowing what kind of response to anticipate from the world around them. They experience feelings of exasperation, as well as disorientation and a loss of control in their lives.

diseases of development, including ADHD and bipolar disorder

Learning impairments and a lack of socialisation skills are potential outcomes of developmental disorders like these. Your kid could grow up in a healthy environment, yet owing to these coexisting disorders, they can still develop anger issues later in life.

Your kid may develop impairments as a result of the illnesses, which will make it more difficult for them to control their urges and frustrations. It's also possible that they feel helpless and inadequate, both of which might contribute to their being angry most of the time.

If your kid has attention deficit hyperactivity disorder (ADHD), he or she may be struggling to meet the unattainable standards set by his classmates. They may easily mistake social signs, be frequently rejected by others, and have a sense of inadequacy as a result of their weak social abilities. Consequently, they may misread social cues.

It's possible that they won't be able to deal with all of these problems. Their furious affect, explosive behaviour, oppositional behaviour, hyperactivity, and impulsiveness may be contributing factors to their anger. Problems related to anger that often arise when your kid has this illness include the following:

The change was abrupt and was accompanied with a heightened awareness before it.

reaches its apex in a short amount of time.

After that, there was a sigh of relief

It is difficult to pinpoint the actual cause of the problem.

Typically disruptive to the lives of the family

It is probable that the following will be true of your kid if he or she suffers from developmental disorders:

Think in a steadfast manner.

Maintain a modest degree of frustration.

Easily get overstimulated and overcome with emotion

Struggle to adapt to shifting priorities and plans

It is more likely that you will experience the outbursts at school than at home.

Concern or worry

Your kid might be suffering from significant anxiety that is going undiagnosed, which is causing him or her to be irritable and defiant. Your kid may be battling with things that put too much strain on him or her, particularly while they are in school. If your child suffers from anxiety, this may be the case.

It's possible that this may prompt him or her to lash out and have recurrent outbursts. Because of the overpowering anxiety, the person may make the decision to refrain from engaging in a certain activity.

Now that you have a better grasp of the factors that contribute to anger, let us examine the strategies that may be used to control anger.

The Most Pervasive Misconceptions Regarding Angry Behavior

Imagine a person who has difficulty controlling their rage. You probably immediately had an image pop into your head of someone yelling at the top of their lungs, fighting with anybody and everyone, and damaging things all about their home. Although this may be the case in certain circumstances, the reality of the matter is that anger may or may not have any direct connection to the decision to verbally or physically lash out at someone. Because of this, as well as a number of other frequent misunderstandings regarding anger, the emotion is very little understood, which makes it challenging to treat. In order to avoid making your anger worse by using ineffective treatments, you first need to have a solid understanding of what anger really is.

It is a common misconception that anger is a bad feeling. Even though rage is a complicated emotion, there are times when it serves a beneficial purpose. Imagine a situation in which a parent feels the need to become a little bit upset with a young kid because the youngster is developing a poor pattern of behaviour and would not listen otherwise. The expression of rage will not only eradicate the issue at hand but will also lead to an improvement in the quality of the relationship. As a result, rage need not necessarily take a destructive form. When it goes out of control, though, it transforms into the second category.

Is it true that one cannot exercise control over their anger? Not true. Even if anger cannot be completely eradicated, the way in which you choose to cope with it is totally up to you. The answer is that anger management can't show you how to stop becoming angry altogether. You may, however, learn how to cope with stress in a manner that is psychologically healthy for you and others around you, and this can be a benefit to both of you.

Getting rage out in the open is helpful - Yes, punching a pillow or yelling at the top of your lungs may provide you with a momentary release from the sensations of aggravation. Having said that, does this indicate that the primary issue has been resolved? Does this indicate that the anger will not surface again? Because the answer to both of these questions is "no," it follows that releasing one's anger vocally or physically may not be the most effective method to go with controlling one's anger. Yes, even the most typical methods of venting that you have heard of might be more harmful than good in some circumstances.

It is possible that you were instructed to disregard the flaws of others and to just dismiss anger if it ever comes to you. If this was the case, you may have been taught that anger can be eliminated by repressing it. However, despite popular belief, stuffing your anger will not make it go away on its own. It will just allow it to exist in that state and, with or without your understanding, transform it into something that is far more hazardous. It is possible for it to lead to a number of psychological disorders in addition to damaging relationships.

This is a popular assumption that is very erroneous, since anger management is all about knowing how to express anger, but in a controlled manner that is forceful without having to turn to extreme ways. Anger management is all about knowing how to express anger in a way that is assertive without having to resort to extreme measures.

It is not a bad thing to become angry if it motivates you to get things done. For example, you yell at your colleagues, and as a result, they get their job done on time. Even if this is true, engaging in behaviour like this is not in any way beneficial to your health. These kinds of strategies are likely to negatively impact your relationships with other people in a direct manner. People will be reluctant to open up to you and will take a defensive stance rather than try to find areas of agreement with you, despite the fact that it may make them fearful. At work or at home, they will merely find for ways to get through the assignment in order to escape your displeasure. It is not because they understand your point of view, which may be detrimental in the long term.

The expression of anger may differ from person to person, and in certain instances, even if someone has never spoken out loud in anger, they may be in desperate need of counselling. Anger is fine as long as the physical or verbal hostility is not severe. There are instances when you or a loved one may not be able to determine if what you or they are experiencing is anger or whether it requires urgent care. For this reason, you need to be aware of the frequent ways in which your anger may be presenting itself in order to properly evaluate how serious the situation is becoming. The following is a list of less common varieties of anger; if you recognise any of them in yourself and believe you have a handle on them, you should think carefully about using anger management techniques.

Pleasantly relaxing

Even though it can seem foolish at first, doing breathing exercises can really be quite useful. If you discover that you have difficulty completing a breathing exercise on your own, you may want to explore browsing YouTube for videos that might assist you in learning the methods and guide you through the exercise. There are some films that will guide you through a breathing exercise that lasts for five to ten minutes, and they may even include soothing music or pictures to accompany the practise. You may find these videos online.

Deep breathing is a component of many different breathing exercises. It is possible to improve the depth of your breath by visualising drawing it from your diaphragm (or your stomach), which may help you breathe more deeply. If you take a number of deep, slow breaths over a short period of time, you may find that your heart rate decreases, your blood pressure falls, your hands remain steady, and you experience an overall sense of calmness.

During physical activity, some individuals find it useful to tell oneself affirmative words such as "Take it easy," "Breathe in, breathe out," or "Relax," such as "Take it easy," "Breathe in, breathe out," or "Relax." They might listen to music that has been shown to have a soothing impact, such as music composed in a classical style or even music performed by their favourite performer.

Visualisation exercises that help you relax might also be effective. A lot of individuals have no trouble imagining a "happy place" or a utopia of some kind. Simply shut your eyes, take some deep breaths, and picture yourself at your favourite spot, far away from whatever is bothering you right now. This should help. This action has the potential to produce a state of extreme tranquilly when carried out.

In the heat of the moment, these tools are of tremendous assistance; but, it is as necessary to engage in activities that promote relaxation on a daily or weekly basis. This can assist in relieving tension and will prevent your rage from becoming out of hand.

You may want to make yoga a regular part of your routine. You may alleviate stress, relax, and achieve inner calm by doing yoga. It is also a physically beneficial practise to engage in. Practising yoga can help you burn calories, develop your flexibility, and tone your muscles, among other benefits.

If you consistently put in the effort to improve these talents, they will eventually seem like second nature to you. Whenever you notice that your mood is being negatively impacted by anger, you will discover that you immediately begin doing your breathing exercises.

Think About Beginning a New Journal.

There are some individuals who just are not gifted in the art of conversing with other people. They could be concerned that others will judge them negatively if they acknowledge that they are angry, or they might not have anybody around who would listen to them and comprehend what is going on. Either way, they can be reluctant to disclose their emotions of anger to others. since of this, the affected individuals may experience significant levels of frustration since they are unsure of where they may turn to vent all of their hatred and anger in a secure way.

Keeping a journal is a useful practise in this regard. Journaling is a safe and extremely effective method for you to go through your emotions and get them out before they start to damage you. If you are not good at expressing your thoughts to someone else, or if you are unclear about who to speak to, journaling is a way for you to go through your feelings and get them out before they start to harm you. You will be able to jot everything down without having to worry about how other people may perceive you as a result of your actions.

Using this method, you are free to write about anything that interests you, and it is perfectly OK for you to utilise your computer in order to make the writing process simpler. Then, the next time that you are feeling indignant or really furious, you should write down everything that is making you feel that way. When you are writing in your diary, you should make sure that you are being absolutely honest about what you are putting down, even if doing so can give the impression that you are pessimistic. Because this is a private diary and no one else will read it until you want to share it to them, it is imperative that every detail be recorded as precisely as possible.

After you have had some time to jot down the ideas that have been going through your head, it is time to relive the experience in its entirety. You need to find out what actions you can do to resolve this specific issue, and then you need to learn how to prevent it in the future. This might assist to prepare you for some of the things that could happen to you later on in life.

This notebook is designed to assist you in a variety of different ways. To begin, some individuals are better able to control their anger if they can let it out in some way, and this applies to both children and adults. You will discover that merely writing down the facts is incredibly therapeutic and will help you feel better. If you do this, you will feel better. In addition, if you find yourself in a position that is analogous in the future, and it causes you to feel irritated, you may consult the diary to see how you may have dealt with a similar circumstance in the past. This will provide you with some helpful examples of what you might do if you find yourself in a similar circumstance in the future.

You may also use this diary to burn away all of those furious thoughts, which is still another thing you can do with it. It is time to burn it after you have finished putting down your thoughts and what has made you so upset. You may either take a little flame and burn those ideas up or toss them into the fire to get rid of them. Even though you are, in all actuality, dealing with nothing more than a piece of paper, many individuals find that writing their ideas down on paper and then seeing them disappear as the paper burns is a very therapeutic activity. They both seem to be extinguishing their fury at the same moment as well.

The Influence Of Having Compassion For Oneself

Although this may seem to be a natural motivator for you to change, there is a risk that might stymie your progress even before you begin. This risk is associated with allowing feelings of shame and self-criticism to demoralise you to the point where you give up attempting to control your anger.

You are in luck since you have access to a fantastic tool that will assist you in remaining on track. Self-compassion is the technique in question, and if you make it a habit to practise it on a daily basis, you will find that it has a profound impact on your life. Developing greater self-compassion may not seem to be required at first glance, but it is in fact the missing piece that will complete the puzzle of your anger management programme and make it possible for you to achieve long-term success.

After you've completely lost your cool, how do you think you should feel about yourself? If you're like the majority of individuals who struggle with controlling their anger, you undoubtedly have a poor opinion of yourself. You may even mentally relive the action over and again, berating yourself with nasty terms each time you do so. I can confirm that I have done this. Even though it made me feel bad about myself, I believed it was vital to teach myself a lesson in spite of the fact that it had that effect.

I was under the impression that the most effective method to curtail my future fits of rage was to be harsh on and condemn myself. On the other hand, I started to evaluate the results of my self-critical behaviour and discovered that it was not assisting me in keeping my cool under pressure. In point of fact, as I grew more conscious of the patterns of my anger, I came to the realisation that the practise of constantly criticisingmyself was having a significant negative impact on my mental wellbeing.

The Many Faces of Anger in Chapter II

There are many distinct expressions of rage. Because everyone of us responds differently to a given circumstance, it is quite challenging to classify them all as belonging to the same category of rage. Take some time to familiarise yourself with the following names and explanations of the most frequent forms of rage so that you may have a better grasp on the subject. It's possible that you'll locate one that appears to match your condition right now.

Anger that is Behavioural

This kind of rage is brought on by a specific stimulus, which may take the form of an item or a person, and it may lead to aggressive behaviour. This sort of fury may result in abuse of any kind, including verbal or physical violence.

An individual's "fight or flight" reaction to any kind of perceived threat is at the root of their behavioural fury. This might also be the consequence of environmental influences, ongoing disappointments, or a pessimistic outlook on the situation. This may lead to a person being highly dissatisfied with particular things or other people in his or her immediate surroundings, as well as being afraid of, or hostile towards, those things or other people.

Aggravated Anger

People who suffer from chronic anger may seem to be irrationally angry at all times. These individuals do not have a single common precipitating factor. Because of the hormonal imbalance that may occur in their brains, older men are more likely to be affected by this condition, which can lead them to become irritable.

This kind of rage isn't something that exclusively happens to older males. This kind of rage may also affect young individuals of either gender and can manifest itself in different ways. This is typically the outcome of many disappointments and a sense of despair or desperation without any result or reprieve.

Anger that is Healthy for You

You've participated in constructive anger if you've ever been so enraged that it drove you to support a certain movement or cause as a result of your anger. This is generally the outcome of individuals being exhausted with a certain circumstance and wanting a change.

In contrast to the other forms of rage, this method of dealing with anger management is characterised by a strong emphasis on proactivity. The drawback of this kind of anger is that when individuals who suffer from this form of anger get together, there is a high propensity for the situation to escalate into a physical conflict. This is a negative aspect of this form of anger.

The Angry Spirit

People who hold prominent positions in society or have a strong moral standing in the society are often the ones that exhibit this kind of fury. People who have this mindset consider themselves to be in a league of their own in comparison to others and, as a result, are convinced that they are always acting in the most moral manner possible. When other individuals cross a specific boundary or disobey certain norms, it may often set off this form of fury in people.

Anger Fueled by Paranoia

Because of the condition of uncertainty that it puts a person in, paranoia often results in paranoid fury in that individual. People who suffer from paranoia tend to keep a watchful eye on their surroundings and maintain a high level of scepticism about everything in their immediate environment.

Because it stems from a mental impairment, this kind of fury cannot be contained or managed in any way. The severity of the paranoia that a person is experiencing might also cause them to experience an escalation of this kind of fury. Additionally, this might be brought on by the use of mind-altering substances by the individual who is suffering from paranoid rage.

Anger Taken in a Passive-Aggressive Manner

This kind of rage is quite prevalent and may often be seen in the majority of individuals. A lack of control in social circumstances often results in the manifestation of both hostile and passive-aggressive behaviours in the individual involved. A veiled statement, which is analogous to a sarcastic remark directed against a specific individual, is an example of this kind of speech.

When people are unhappy in their social or professional lives, they often experience this kind of fury. This may happen either at work or in social settings. An office setting is a good example since it requires individuals of diverse levels of responsibility to collaborate.

Fury Suppressed in Oneself

It is assumed that keeping one's emotions in control or keeping rage buried might lead to cardiac arrest or cancer, both of which are considered to be serious health risks. People who suppress their rage often display little to no outward signs that they are going through any kind of emotional or mental distress. Someone looking at them could perhaps get the impression that they are exceptionally patient individuals. What other people do not realise is that those who suffer from the condition of suppressed anger are churning with rage on the inside, and they are a time bomb waiting to go off. Their ire may sometimes surface in the form of passive-aggressive fury shown in the form of snarky reactions to the concerns of other individuals.

Anger Motivated by Guilt

Anger motivated by feelings of shame is experienced by the majority of individuals after experiencing an uncomfortable circumstance. Frustration is likely to ensue if one is unprepared to respond appropriately to situations like these. The outward manifestation of rage that is rooted in shame is often either walking away or stewing in place.

Environment may also play a role in the development of rage that is motivated by feelings of shame. A person who is being bullied by other individuals is an excellent illustration. This might result in suppressed sentiments, which, in the end, can lead to rage based on guilt because of the seeming inability to defend and advocate for one's own self-interests.

Anger that is Caused by Oneself

This is the most dangerous kind of fury because it may lead to someone inflicting bodily damage on themselves. When unregulated, a person has the potential to do significant bodily injury to himself. This kind of fury often leads to self-harming behaviours such as cutting, beating oneself up, starving oneself, or overeating. There is a very wide variety of triggers that might set someone off on a path of rage that they have brought upon themselves. It might be anything from a broken heart to the plain irritation of not being able to do anything you set out to do.

People who display this kind of rage should seek professional counselling without delay in order to prevent inflicting more harm to themselves than they already have done.

www.ingramcontent.com/pod-product-compliance
Lightning Source LLC
Chambersburg PA
CBHW050419120526
44590CB00015B/2021